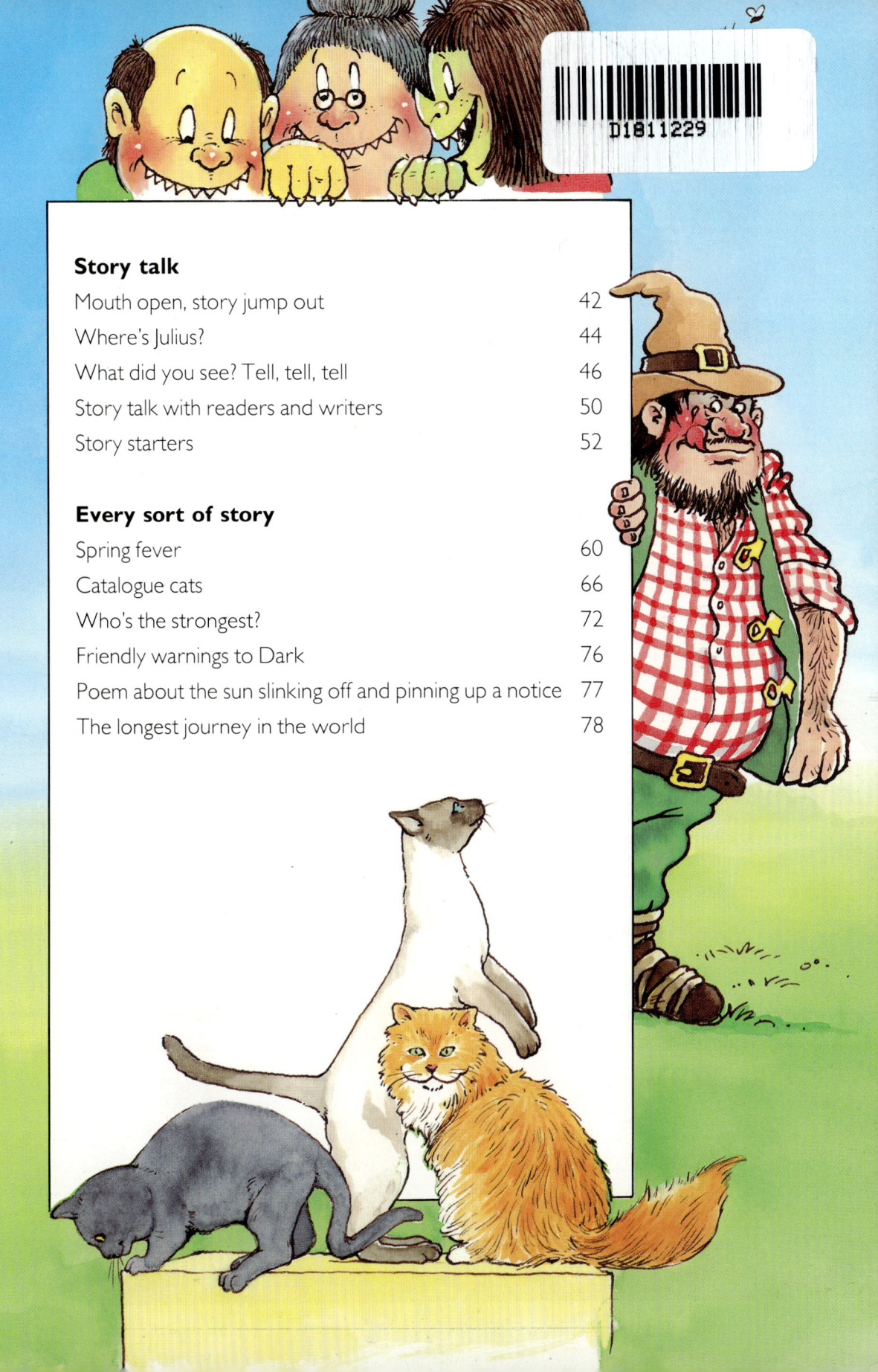

Story talk

Every sort of story

PICKING UP CLUES — READ YOUR SCHOOL

Book Corner

Quiet Please

Story Books

Come and find Books about birds. They have a green label. Their code number is 598

Some books have a contents page at the front and an index at the back to help you.

Sir Tim battles against the dragon by 3F

by 3F

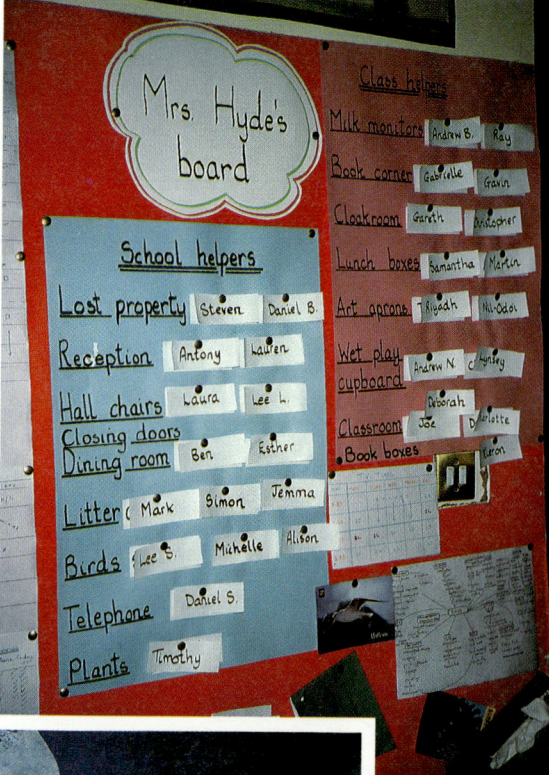

Mrs. Hyde's board

School helpers

Lost property — Steven — Daniel B.

Reception — Antony — Lauren

Hall chairs — Laura — Lee L.

Closing doors

Dining room — Ben — Esther

Litter — Mark — Simon — Jemma

Birds — Lee S. — Michelle — Alison

Telephone — Daniel S.

Plants — Timothy

Class helpers

Milk monitors — Andrew B. — Ray

Book corner — Gabrielle — Gavin

Cloakroom — Gareth — Christopher

Lunch boxes — Samantha — Martin

Art aprons — Aliyaah — Nii-Odoi

Wet play cupboard — Andrew N. — Chynley

Classroom — Joe — Deborah — Charlotte

Book boxes — Turan

song thrush

bird table

blue-tit

bird feeder

pigeon

crow

robin

This is a collage of part of our school grounds where we have been watching for birds.

sparrow

Classroom 3

Mrs. L. Hyde

Welcome

Please come in

THE BALLOON LAUNCH.

Monks Orchard are 50

way!

up!

Balloon Launch.

In a big green field
Excitement fills the air,
The children wondering when
they'll get there.
One to Scotland,
One to France,
Surely there is a chance!
As voices chanting
From ten to one,
Yes,
Now the lift-off has begun!
Up they soar,
Some fall to the floor!
Some stick to a tree,
All the children want to see,
But mostly they stare at the
brilliant sky,
As the pretty colours go
sailing by.

Natalie Tomecki 5?

BALLOONS

Up in the air and out of
sight
The balloons fly higher like
a kite,
Soaring up, straight past
the sun
It's blinding my eyes but
still it's fun.
I take one last look at the
tiny dots
Now I realise there are lots,
There's now not a single
one to see;
They've floated far away
from me.

Sarah Totterdell 5B.

Around The Area.

Why not send them a greeting

Look at the photographs on these pages. Read all the notices and messages.

Imagine that a group of children are coming to spend a day in your school. Draw or write a notice for each of the following areas. Think about what would be interesting and helpful for your visitors to look at or read.

classroom   library or book corner
hall   cloakroom
dining room   playground

5

LOOK OUT!

In pairs or small groups talk about the notice which you think might be drawn or written in each of the pictures on these pages. On a piece of paper draw or write all the notices you have talked about. Read your notices aloud to the rest of the class.

Were any of them warning notices?

BEWARE OF THE GIANT

Here is the beginning of a famous story, *The selfish giant*, by Oscar Wilde. In it you will read about a notice which the giant put up in his garden.

Every afternoon, as they were coming from school, the children used to go and play in the Giant's garden.

It was a large lovely garden, with soft green grass. Here and there over the grass stood beautiful flowers like stars, and there were twelve peach-trees that in the spring-time broke out into delicate blossoms of pink and pearl, and in the autumn bore rich fruit. The birds sat on the trees and sang so sweetly that the children used to stop their games in order to listen to them. "How happy we are here!" they cried to each other.

One day the Giant came back. He had been to visit his friend the Cornish ogre, and had stayed with him for seven years.

After the seven years were over he had said all that he had to say, for his conversation was limited, and he determined to return to his own castle. When he arrived he saw the children playing in the garden.

"What are you doing here?" he cried in a very gruff voice, and the children ran away.

"My own garden is my own garden," said the Giant; "anyone can understand that, and I will allow nobody to play in it but myself." So he built a high wall all round it and put up a notice-board saying: TRESPASSERS WILL BE PROSECUTED.

What do you feel about the children going into the garden without permission?

Perhaps if they wrote a letter to the giant telling him why they played in his garden, he might change his mind. Would you like to finish this one for them?

FRIENDLY WARNINGS

After the giant's unfriendly warning to the children, here is a friendly warning to grass. It's by Robert Froman.

LISTEN GRASS, TAKE IT EASY. DON'T GROW TOO TALL, THEY'LL JUST BRING IN A LAWN MOWER AND CUT YOU DOWN SHORT SEE? I TOLD YOU THEY WOULD

A group of children and their teacher had fun making up their own friendly warnings.

This is the children's message to ice:

Listen ICE, don't make people slip or else they will put salt on you and make you MELT

They spent a long time talking about how to write their words down. Can you find another way?

Their teacher made a joke out of his warning notice. Here it is:

LISTEN ICE NO MORE JOKES, YOU'VE CRACKED ENOUGH ALREADY

Now you make up your own friendly warning notice which begins with the word LISTEN.

Here are some ideas to start you thinking, talking and writing:

LISTEN Wasp

LISTEN Tadpole

LISTEN Dark

LISTEN Baby

You have thought and talked about how you can write notices down. Here is another one which you may have seen:

And here are the same words:

PRIVATE?
NO. SWIMMING
ALLOWED

PRIVATE
NO SWIMMING
ALLOWED

Read both notices several times. Do they mean the same?

Can you make up any more notices like these?

11

FRIENDLY INVITATIONS

Have you ever thought that the cover of a book is a kind of notice; a friendly invitation to guess what the inside story might be about?

Look at the titles and book covers on these pages.

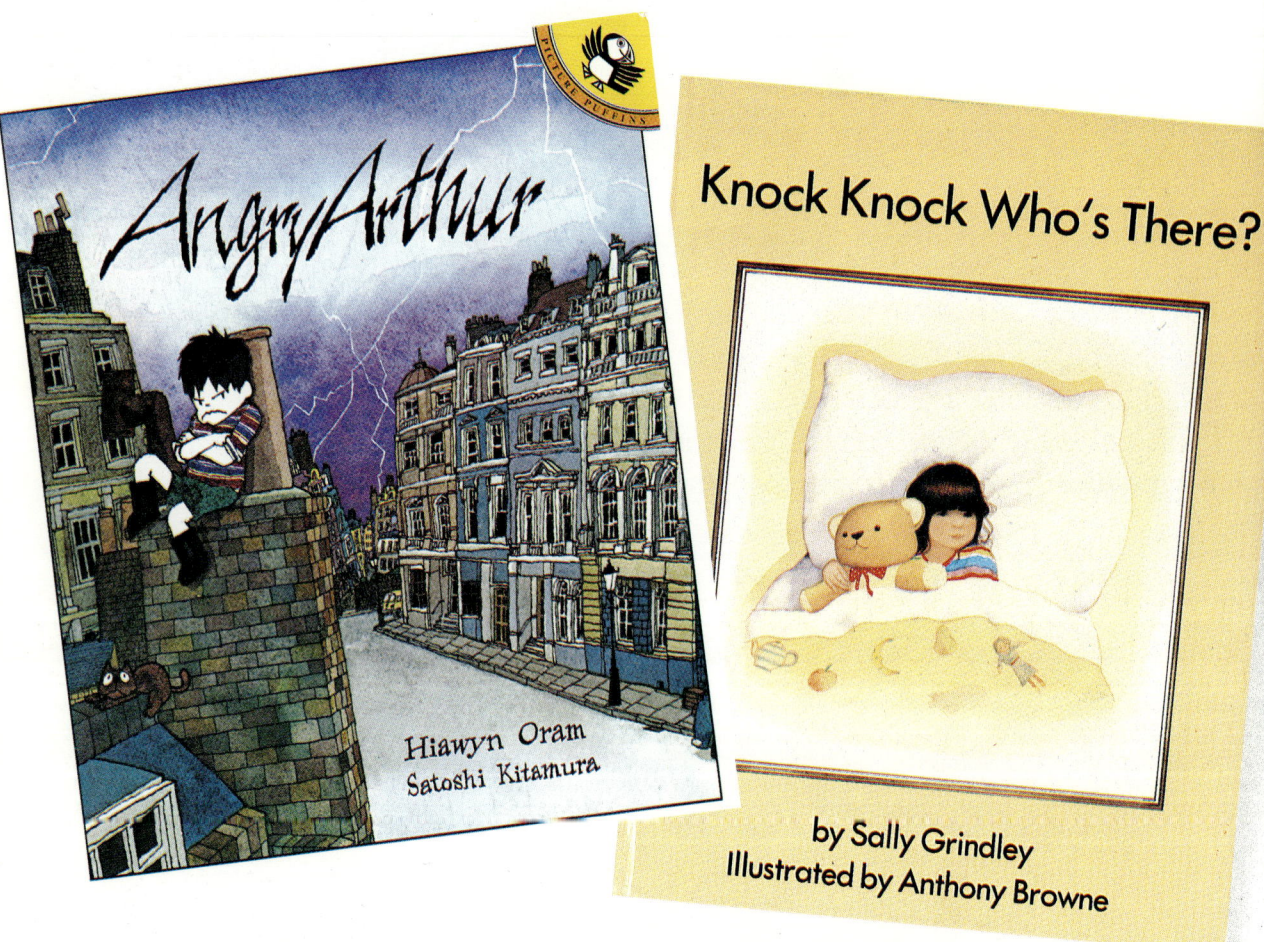

What do you think each book might be about?

Which one would you most like to read?

Tell your story of the cover to a friend.

You can find out how some of these stories start by looking on pages 52–59.

BRINGING THE RAIN TO KAPITI PLAIN

by Verna Aardema

illustrated by Beatriz Vidal

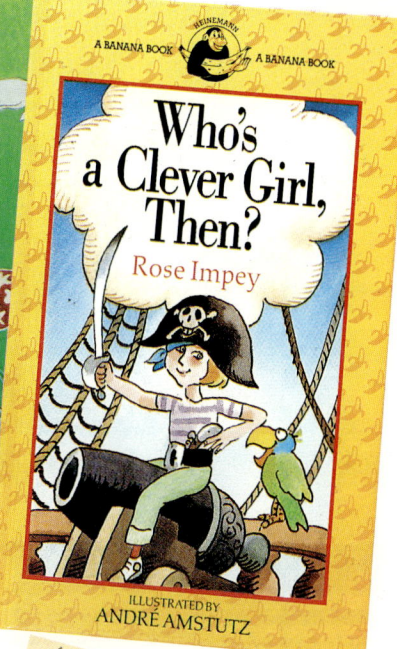

Who's a Clever Girl, Then?

Rose Impey

ILLUSTRATED BY
ANDRÉ AMSTUTZ

WHODUNNIT?

CAROLINE BROWNE

Story told by Helen Cresswell

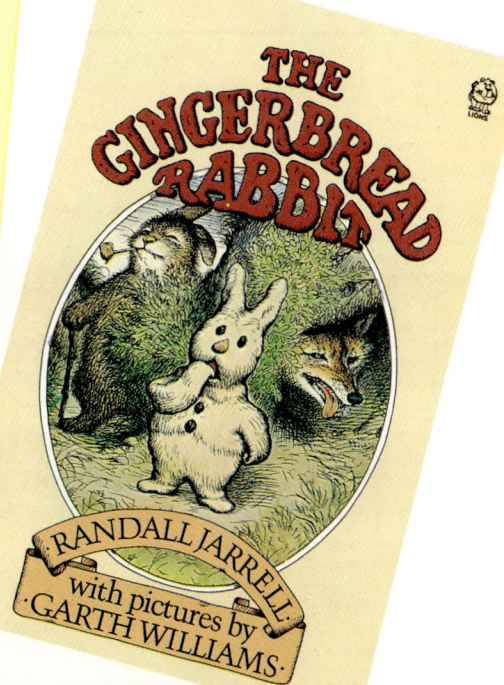

THE GINGERBREAD RABBIT

RANDALL JARRELL

with pictures by
GARTH WILLIAMS

PICTURE CLUES

These pictures come from the beginning of a story which has not got any words. It doesn't need them. The pictures tell the story. It's called *The hunter and the animals,* and it's by Tomie de Paola.

A group of children your age looked at all the pictures in the book. As they told the story, their teacher wrote it down for them. You can see photographs of the children too.

It is acorn time in the woods.
Squirrels are hunting for their winter food.
Rabbits and foxes are playing in the sunshine.
In a house near to the woods
a boy woke up and yawned.
He pulled on his boots and
he pulled on his trousers.
He pushed his arms through
the sleeves of his jacket
and then he straightened
his hat so that the feather
pointed forwards.

The last thing the boy did
was to stretch for his rifle.

As the boy came walking into the woods,
a bird spread the news
that a boy was coming
with a rifle on his shoulder.
When the animals heard,
they all ran and hid.

The squirrels left their acorns,
the rabbits stopped playing,
the foxes and the deer ran far
away.

15

The boy aimed for the foxes
and the squirrels and the rabbits
and the foxes and the birds
but he did not kill anything.

At the end of the day he fell asleep
against a tree.
All the animals and the birds came out,
took the rifle and his bag of water.
They picked leaves and branches
from the trees.

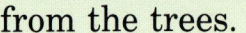

When the boy woke up, he was frightened.
The moon began to rise and the night came.
He looked around but he couldn't find the way home.
And he cried.

The animals felt sorry for him, so they brought
him fruit and gave him back his rifle and
his hat and his bag.
They led the way out of the woods to the boy's hut.
When they all got home the boy stopped and
turned his rifle towards the birds and animals.
They were afraid until they saw him crack it
hard across his knee.
The rifle broke into two pieces.
From now on they were friends and they
played happily ever after.

This story was made up by:

Ozma Rajah   Eric Koranteng
Michaela Berney   David Allen
Danielle Vian   Paapa Dougan

What did you enjoy about this story?
   Draw some pictures to go with the middle or end parts of the story.

17

This book cover and these nine pictures come from the middle of a story without words.

Begin by giving the little girl a name and saying why she could not get to sleep. Now tell the rest of the story.

Moonlight Jan Ormerod

Did you think about what the little girl and her mum might be saying to each other?

What happens if we start the story with picture
number 5 . . .

. . . and continue the story using the pictures in
this order:

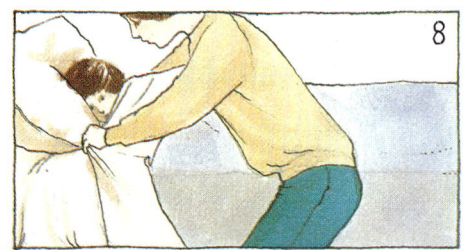

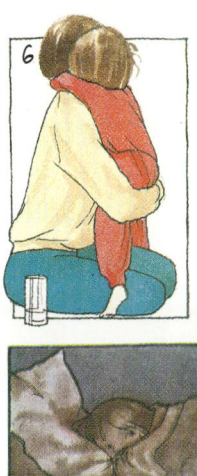

Tell your new story and carry on with it after picture number 5.

Ask someone to help you write your story. What are you going to
call it?

Can you find some other books in your classroom or library which tell
their stories through pictures? Make a list of them.

WORDS AND PICTURES

On the way home is a very funny story told in pictures and words.
   This is part of the story, which you can enjoy reading in pairs. One of you could read all the words which Claire says and the other one could read all the rest.

Then Claire met her friend Amarjit.
"Look at my bad knee," said Claire.
"How did you do it?" asked Amarjit.

"*Well*," said Claire, "there was a huge, hungry crocodile,

and it came lumbering out of the canal as I passed by, and it tried to pull m
into the water!

But I crammed a piece of wood between its jaws and it was *so*

oss that it knocked me over with
s tail, and *that's* how I got my bad knee". "How dreadful!" said Amarjit.

he cover of the book gives us clues about
ome of the other stories which Claire makes
o . . . .

Look at this cover and make a list of every-
ing you can see around Claire. Then
hoose one of the cover clues and make up
our own "fib" story to tell how Claire got
er bad knee. You could begin with the
ords:

hen Claire met her friend Steven and
aid . . . ."

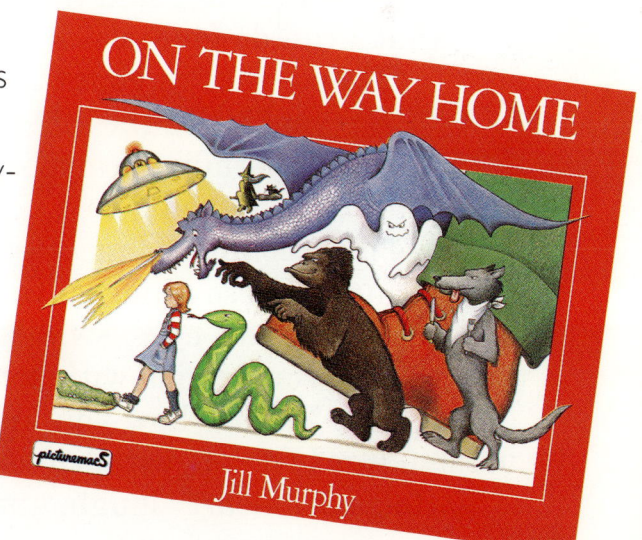

ON THE WAY HOME

picturemacs

Jill Murphy

21

ARE YOU A GOOD DETECTIVE?

Read or listen to this story:

In the meantime the rabbit had run along the path as fast as *he* could go, but in next to no time he was out of breath again. His heart thumped so . . . that he said to himself: "I just can't run any more, I've *got* to find some place to hide." Just then at the bottom of a big mossy rock, . . . he saw the entrance to a little cave. By it was sitting a beautiful furry red animal with a white breast and a beautiful big plumy red tail. "If only he'd let me hide in his cave," thought the rabbit . . . .

"Ah, good morning, good morning," the other said.

The rabbit said: "I – I –"

"Why, my dear fellow," said the other, "you're completely out of breath . . . . Come, sit down here beside me in the shade!"

The rabbit sat down on the bank of moss; he was already beginning to get his breath.

"Now tell me," said the beautiful red animal, "what is there that I can do for you?" . . .

"They – they're going to eat me," the rabbit said. "They're –"

"*Eat* you!" cried the other. "Eat *you!* But who could be guilty of such an enormity? I myself have been, for almost more years than I can remember, a vegetarian; but the thought that even the most confirmed meat-eater could bear to gobble up so young, so innocent, so tender a rabbit as yourself . . ." – he brushed a tear out of his eyes, swallowed, and licked his lips – . . . .

"Are you friends with some rabbits yourself?" asked the rabbit. "Is that how you know I'm a rabbit?"

"Am I friends with some rabbits myself?" repeated the other. He gave a hearty laugh, and waved his paw. "Is that how I know

22

you're a rabbit?" He gave an even heartier laugh, and waved both paws. "Why, my dear fellow, *what do you think I am myself?*"

The rabbit said: "You mean that you –"

"I mean that I'm a rabbit! A red rabbit, I admit. A long-tailed rabbit, I admit. A short-eared rabbit, I admit. But a *rabbit* – and a rabbit that would lay down his life for the sake of a brother rabbit!"

The gingerbread rabbit was so overjoyed that he could hardly speak. Tears came into his eyes, so that the two raisins got bigger and shinier and almost looked like grapes. "To think that at last I've met another rabbit!" he exclaimed.

"But tell me," said the other, "what is it that's trying to eat you? A wolf? A – not a dog, I hope?" . . .

"A giant!" said the gingerbread rabbit. "A giant that's going to cook me alive!"

"To *cook* you!" said the other rabbit. "What an absurd – that is to say, what an atrocious thing to do!"

"Awful, awful!" exclaimed the gingerbread rabbit. "And I can't keep on running, I'm so tired . . . . Could I – would you let me hide inside your lovely cave?"

Can you name and draw the creature that the rabbit meets?
Can you spot the fibs that the creature tells the rabbit?
Tell the story of what might happen next.
Does the rabbit go into the cave?
The cover of this book is shown on page 13. It may help you.

FIND THE MISSING WORDS

Read this poem by Brian Patten and talk about it in your group.
Choose a word for each of the empty spaces.

Someone stole the

While I was taking a short _ nap
   someone stole the _,
I should have spun round like a _herine wheel
   when someone stole the _.
But I was too slow to _ch them,
   when someone stole the _.

   Now the _amaran can't float,
     because someone stole the _.
   And the _erpillar can't crawl,
     because someone stole the _.
   And the _aract can't fall,
     because someone stole the _.

It was not me and it was not you
   but it is _egorically true,
And if you were to ask me
   I'd say it was a _astrophe
That someone's stolen the _.

When you have talked about the words which could fill the spaces, write
out the poem and read it aloud.
   Find out the meaning of any words you do not know.

Read this poem by Olive Dehn and talk about it in your group.

Use all the picture clues to help you choose one word for each of the eight empty spaces in the poem.

In the middle of the city
Is an __ space called a __
It is difficult for us to do what we like there
Even after dark.

In the middle of the Park there is a statue,
A huge man made of __
We are not allowed to climb his legs or scribble on his trousers,
He has to be left alone.

In the middle of the grass there is some __
Surrounded by an asphalt path;
We are __ __ to fish or throw stones into it
Or swim or take a bath.

In the __ of the water is an island
Full of __ things.
But none of us has ever set foot upon it
Because none of us has wings.

Write out the poem, putting in the words you have chosen.

Read it aloud to the other groups in your class.

Give the poem a title. Write down all your ideas on a large piece of paper. Underline the one you like best.

Your teacher will tell you the title and the words that the poet used.

Read the poem again, putting in the words that the poet chose. Are you surprised or disappointed by the title and any of these words?

IF AT FIRST YOU DO NOT SEE

HAMBURGER?
ICE CREAM?

How many pictures do you think there are on this page? Look ... and look again!

If you are thinking that you might like to eat this tasty hamburger ... think again ... it might be just about to eat you!

Fancy an ice cream?

Don't be a clown!

Tell your friends about all the pictures you see on this page.

They are from a book called *If at first you do not see*, by Ruth Brown.

26

DARK IS...

What do you know about bats?

This "batty" poem tells us one thing about a baby bat:

The baby bat
Screamed out in fright,
"Turn on the dark,
I'm afraid of the light."

Shel Silverstein

All baby owls would agree with this young bat ... except one. Have you met *The owl who was afraid of the dark*?

At the beginning of the story, his mother is trying hard to persuade the young owl to go out into the world at night to find out what DARK is really like.

Plop was a baby Barn Owl, and he lived with his Mummy and Daddy at the top of a very tall tree in a field.

Plop was fat and fluffy.

He had a beautiful heart-shaped ruff.

He had enormous, round eyes.

He had very knackety knees.

In fact he was exactly the same as every baby Barn Owl that has ever been – except for one thing.

Plop was afraid of the dark.

"You *can't* be afraid of the dark," said his Mummy. "Owls are *never* afraid of the dark."

"This one is," Plop said.

"But owls are *night* birds," she said.

Plop looked down at his toes. "I don't want to be a night bird," he mumbled. "I want to be a day bird."

27

"You *are* what you *are*," said Mrs Barn Owl firmly.

"Yes, I know," agreed Plop, "and what I are is afraid of the dark."

"Oh dear," said Mrs Barn Owl .... She shut her eyes and tried to think how best she could help Plop not to be afraid. Plop waited.

His mother opened her eyes again. "Plop, you are only afraid of the dark because you don't know about it. What *do* you know about the dark?"

"It's black," said Plop.

"Well, that's wrong for a start. It can be silver or blue or grey or lots of other colours, but almost never black. What else do you know about it?"

"I don't like it," said Plop. "I do not like it AT ALL."

"That's not *knowing* something," said his mother. "That's *feeling* something. I don't think you know anything about the dark at all."

"Dark is nasty," Plop said loudly.

"You don't know that .... I think you had better go down into the world and find out a lot more about the dark before you make up your mind about it."

"Now?" said Plop.

"Now," said his mother.

Plop climbed out of the nest-hole and wobbled along the branch outside. He peeped over the edge. The world seemed to be a very long way down.

"I'm not a very good lander," he said. "I might spill myself."

"Your landing will improve with practice," said his mother. "Look! There's a little boy down there on the edge of the wood collecting sticks. Go and talk to him about it."

"Now?" said Plop.

"Now," said his mother. So Plop shut his eyes, took a deep breath, and fell off his branch.

28

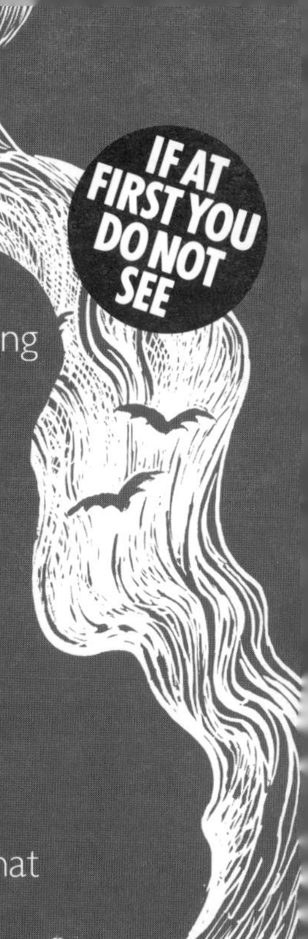
IF AT
FIRST YOU
DO NOT
SEE

IN PAIRS:
One of you is the mother owl and the other is the baby owl.

Use the words from the story or your own words to talk about being afraid of the dark.

This little poem tells you how the baby owl felt about the dark.

The baby h-owl

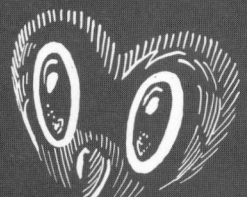

The baby owl
screamed out at night,
"I hate the dark
Bring back the light."

If you read the whole story you will find that the baby owl learns that DARK is:

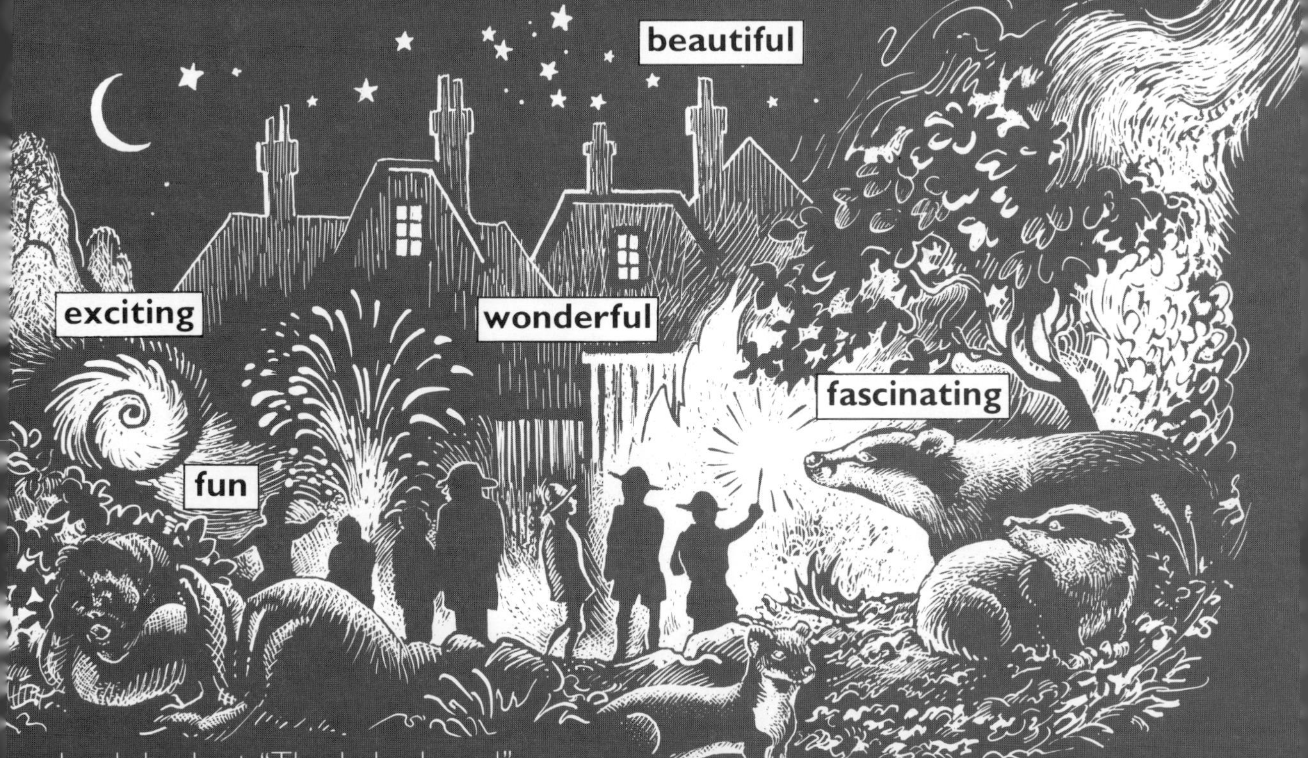
beautiful
exciting
wonderful
fascinating
fun

Look back at "The baby h-owl" verse.

What do you think he might say now that he has changed his mind?

WILD THINGS

You may have met these monsters before in the picture book *Where the wild things are*. But do you know why the artist, Maurice Sendak, drew them like this?

This is the true story behind the pictures.

When he was little, Maurice Sendak remembers looking up from his pram and seeing all his family looking down at him. They looked very ugly. They had big teeth, immense nostrils and very sweaty foreheads. They looked a bit like wild creatures to a small child.

Our artist has drawn what Sendak might have seen when he was a baby.

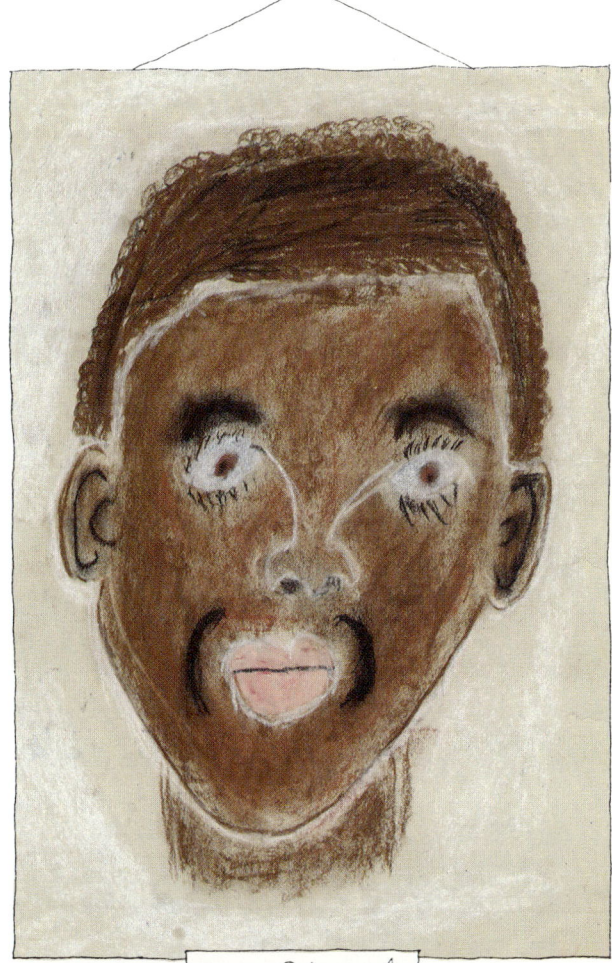

my friend

If you have kept any of your early drawings of your teacher or your family, bring them to share with your class.

Ask a younger child (perhaps a brother or sister) to draw you. Notice the things that look small or big or are missed out of their drawings. Label your drawings and make part of your classroom into a picture gallery, like this.

Miss Starling

my teacher

Ask a grown-up to draw you, or to draw your friend or your brother or sister.

Collect a few of these different drawings and talk about them with your friends. You can write about them too.

31

OUR HAMSTER'S LIFE

Enjoy reading the following poem aloud to each other. You could choose one person in your group to read the words at the end of the poem where the boy imagines what the hamster may be thinking.

Our hamster's life:
there's not much
to it,
not much
to it.

He presses his pink nose
to the door of his cage
and decides for the fifty six
millionth time
that he can't get
through it ....

It's about the most boring
life in the world,
if he only
knew it.
He sleeps and he drinks and he eats.
He eats and he drinks and he sleeps ....

You'd think it would drive him bonkers,
going round and round on his wheel.
It's certainly driving me bonkers,

watching him
do it.

But he may be thinking:
"That boy's life,
there's not much
to it,
not much
to it:

watching a hamster go round on a wheel.
It's driving me bonkers if he only knew it,

watching him
watching me
do it."

Kit Wright

Why does the boy feel sorry for the hamster? Do you feel sorry for the
hamster?

Choose a creature, such as a pet or a picture of an animal, which you
can look at closely.

Draw a picture or write a few lines about what you see. Then draw a
picture or write a few lines about what you think the animal sees when it
looks at you.

33

GERBIL

Look closely at this picture.

Talk about what the gerbil might be *seeing*, *thinking* and *feeling*.

What do you think the child is *seeing*, *thinking* and *feeling*?

Jean Kenward has written a poem to show what she imagines the gerbil in the cage and the child outside are thinking about each other.

Two brown eyes
peep out of the straw,
a quivering nose
and not much more –
a tail as thick
as a bit of string –
he might be a mouse,
or anything.
Tiny, and most
attentive, he
looks as if
he's measuring me.

Two blue eyes
look into my straw:
arms and legs
and a good deal more;
clumsy and huge,
I wonder why
it grows so wide
and it grows so high?
What a peculiar
voice it's got –
it is a PERSON
is it not?

Were any of your ideas the same as hers?

BRIDGET'S STORY

Four people in the first chapter of the story *Bridget and William*, by Jane Gardam say what they think about Bridget wanting a horse now that she has moved to a new farm. They are:

Old Todd, who works on the farm
Bridget's father
Bridget's mother
Bridget

When Bridget was seven she moved to a new farm over in the next dale, and very high.

"Now, face it," Old Todd said to her father, looking round at the heather and the wild sky above it, "it's a grand spot, but it's high. You'll be snowed in maybe once or twice in a winter. It'll do for sheep but it's no place for milk cattle and if you keep a horse it'll have to stand int' stable three parts of the year."

"No horses," said Bridget's father. "One horse eats like five sheep. No profit. No sense in a horse."

"Not a horse for Bridget?" asked Old Todd, "And three grand stables lying empty? Not much else for a little lass up here, high as this."

"Horses is only for townsfolks now," said Bridget's father.

Bridget looked down from the yard gate she was sitting on. The road wound away, down out of sight, into the trees on the one-in-three hill and into the beck. You couldn't see the beck from High Farm but you could hear it rushing. Then you could see the track come out again beyond the beck and wind away and away over the moors.

Far to either side of it there was a dot here and a dot there – low farms with smoke rising. Purple heather came rolling in to the dale bottoms to the sharp edges of bright green fields – squares and oblongs and strips and one field the shape of a boot. Then the track disappeared over a brow near the Saxon Cross and even beyond that you could not see the village. Just a bluebell haze and white clouds hurtling. There were seven white gates along this lovely road. Bridget imagined a horse trotting.

"Think of opening and shutting that lot of gates, coming home of a dark night," said Bridget's mother.

"Council might put in cattle grids," said her father.

"That it might not," said Old Todd. "Cattle grids cost thousands. They'll put in no cattle grids for one high farm. Long gates is best anyways. For horses. All ways over."

"We're having no horses," said Bridget's father. "If Bridget gets lonely I'll buy her a lamb. Maybe two. Then next summer she can sell them and buy four. Learn some farming. Mind, we've not bought this farm yet. It's high. We're still only talking."

"I'd *like* a horse," said Bridget.

"We're having no horse," said her father.

36

Write out ten things which the different people said. Write them in bubbles and put the name of the speaker, like this:

If you keep a horse, it'll have to stand int' stable three parts of the year.

Old Todd

Make sure you write the bubbles in the order that the people spoke the words. Try saying the words in the way that Bridget and the others would have said them. If you get into groups of four, each of you can be one of the four speakers.

Imagine that you are Bridget.
   A friend telephones you to see how you are liking your new farm. Tell your friend about the place and all the reasons why you are not allowed to have a horse.

You could write a letter to a friend from your old school. Tell him or her about the countryside and the new farm. He or she might be interested to know why you want a horse and why you cannot have one.

Later in the story you will find that Bridget receives a birthday letter from her aunt. In it there is a cheque. What do you think will happen next?

A BIT OF GIVE AND TAKE

Bernard Ashley

SCOTT'S STORY

Scott lives in a block of flats in London and he finds a stray kitten inside a large refuse bin.

In groups, read all the words in bubbles. There are three people speaking.

Can you guess who they are? What is Scott's problem?

What's that? Is it alive?

Course it's alive. I saved it. It's a kitten.

A kitten? You don't reckon you're keeping that, do you?

What the devil have you got there?

I am! I saved it from death! He'll die without me!

I can't feed that. I'm hard pushed to feed you two!

He's not keeping that Mum.

Good job! I don't want it crawling on my bed!

Someone's already tried to kill him. He thinks he's safe. He'll never trust no-one no more.

They do it in a box.

What about the mess?

O.K. Great!

Well it's down to you, you hear me?

No cats! No pets except birds in cages and fishes in tanks. It's one of the Council rules - see?

You have read what three people think about the kitten.
Read this chapter from the book to find out who the people are:

"What the devil have you got there?"

Scott's mother bumped into him. She came out of her bedroom behind a dull rainbow of washing and almost smothered the kitten in it.

"What's *that*? Is it alive?"

Sandra screamed. She loved something to scream at. She screamed the way normal people just gave you a look.

"'Course it's alive. I saved it. It's a kitten."

Mrs Turner threw the washing on the floor, there in the hallway.

"A kitten? You don't reckon you're keeping that, do you?"

"He's not keeping that, Mum!"

"I *am*! I saved it from death!" Scott shouted it at them .... "He'll die without me!"

"Good job!" Sandra slammed her bed-room door. "I don't want it crawling on my bed!"

Mrs Turner stood there with a hand on her hip and the other on her forehead. "I can't feed that!" she said. "I'm hard enough pushed to feed you two .... Take it back down, Scott. Let it go, 'fore it starts getting ideas."

Scott cuddled it closer. "No! It won't be no trouble. It can eat what's left-over. Sandra never eats her dinner up."

"I'm not arguing the toss, boy. Do you know the price of a pint of milk? I can't *afford* another mouth to feed."

Scott could see his mother beginning to harden. He had the horrible feeling he was on the way to losing: he did lose sometimes.

39

So he cried. He dropped his lip and started to grizzle. He forced two big tears – both out of the same eye – on to his cheek.

"Someone's already tried to kill him. He thinks he's safe now. He'll never trust no one no more."

Mrs Turner's shoulders drooped. "But what about the mess?"

"They do it in a box. I'll get a box and put some dirt in it. Honest, I won't let him be no trouble, Mum. Mum ..."

Mrs Turner stared at Scott and Scott stared at her.

"Oh, you kids!"

The kitten, not knowing how its life had just been fought for, looked calmly out from Scott's coat ....

"Well, it's down to you, you hear me? I don't want no come-backs."

"O.K.! Great!" And Scott would have cheered, except for scaring his kitten.

But who was his kitten? Scott hadn't thought about that. What was he going to call him?

Suddenly, it came. *Scrap.* Scott stroked its head again. Yes, Scrap. That seemed about right for a kitten saved from the rubbish bin.

Mrs Turner scooped at her washing.

Scott turned to start looking for a box. But before either of them had really made a move, Sandra came bursting out of the kitchen. She had something in her hand. It was the council rent book.

"See this?" she asked, with a false sad look on her face. "See what this says?"

"What's up with you?" Scott didn't pay the rent, did he?

"No cats!" said Sandra. "No pets except birds in cages and fishes in tanks. It's one of the council rules – see?"

Scott stared at the book she was waving in front of him.

"That's why you found him. People have to get shot of pets, or the council has them put to sleep."

Give the parts of Mum, Sandra and Scott to three people in the class. Ask them to read aloud what each person says in the chapter.

Why do you think the council has rules about keeping pets in flats?

Do you agree with them?

Try to get a copy of the book from your local library and read the story to find out whether Scott manages to solve his problem.

STORY TALK

MOUTH OPEN, STORY JUMP OUT

Mouth open
story jump out

I tell you me secret
you let it out

But I don't care
if the world hear
shout it out

Mouth open
story jump out

Besides,
the secret I tell you
wasn't even true
so you can shout
till you blue

So boo
mouth open
story jump out

Read this poem by John Agard aloud round your group or class.

Make up an impossible short story about something that you pretend has happened to you.

For ideas look back to Claire's story of how she hurt one knee on pages 20 and 21.

It could be a story, like this one, about why you were late for school one day:

"I was just leaving my house when this blue kangaroo asked me if I'd like a lift. I climbed into her pouch and we hopped off ...."

Think about your story before telling it to a friend. When you are ready, sit in a circle in your group. Say the first verse all together:

"Mouth open
Story jump out"

Now one of you tell your pretend story. When you come to the end, all say together:

"Mouth open
Story jump out"

Then the next story is told, and so on until everyone has had a turn.

   "Tall" is the name given to stories like yours that everyone knows couldn't possibly be true. Perhaps your class would like to make a:

TALL Story Book.
If you do write down your TALL stories, remember to keep them amazing and short!

WHERE'S JULIUS?

Julius Troutbeck is one boy who takes his adventures very seriously. He never stops pretending, not even at meal times. Here his mother and father are getting lunch ready. His mother asks where Julius is.

"For lunch there is cheese salad with celery and tomato and an orange for pudding if you want it.
Where's Julius?"

"Julius says he cannot have lunch with us just at the moment because he is cooling the hippopotamuses in the Lombo Bombo River in Central Africa, with buckets of muddy water."

So Mr Troutbeck took the tray with the cheese salad with celery and tomato and the orange for pudding to Africa where Julius was pouring buckets of muddy water on the hippopotamuses, to keep them cool.

Later, his father is preparing supper.

"I've got the lamb casserole for supper out of the oven and the potatoes in their jackets and broccoli with butter on top and for afterwards there is roly-poly pudding.

Where's Julius?"

"Julius says he cannot have supper with us just at the moment because he is digging a hole in order to get to the other side of the world."

44

So Mrs Troutbeck took the lamb casserole, the potatoes in their jackets and broccoli with butter on top and the roly-poly pudding for afterwards to where Julius was digging his hole.

STORY TALK

These adventures come from the book *Where's Julius?* by John Burningham. Imagine that Julius has come into your story circle. What exciting tales does he have to share with you about his journey to the other side of the world? Think of some adventures and tell them round your group. Each of you in turn can be Julius.

Now think about what *you* like to eat. What are you busy doing when someone says "Where's . . .?"

Make up your own menu and adventure, and tell it round your group. Perhaps you would like to make a neat copy of a "Julius" story for your class TALL Story Book. Add some drawings if you like.

WHAT DID YOU SEE?
TELL, TELL, TELL

Here is another poem for you to enjoy reading aloud round your class.

A new family's coming to live next door to me.
I looked in the moving van to see what I could see.
What did you see?
Tell, tell, tell.

Well,
I saw a frying pan in the moving van.
What else did you see?
Tell, tell, tell.

Well,
I saw a rocking chair and a stuffed teddy bear
and a frying pan in the moving van.
What else did you see?
Tell, tell, tell.

Well,
I saw a rug for the floor
and a boat with an oar
and a rocking chair
and a stuffed teddy bear
and a frying pan
in the moving van.
What else did you see?
Tell, tell, tell.

Well, I saw a leather boot and a
   basket of fruit
and a rug for the floor and a
   boat with an oar
and a rocking chair and a stuffed
   teddy bear
and a frying pan in the moving van.
   What else did you see?
   Tell, tell, tell.

Well, I saw a TV set and a
   Ping-Pong net
and a leather boot and a basket of fruit
and a rug for the floor and a boat with an oar
and a rocking chair and a stuffed teddy bear
and a frying pan in the moving van.
   What else did you see?
   Tell, tell, tell.

Well, I saw a steamer trunk and a double-decker bunk
and a TV set and a Ping-Pong net
and a leather boot and a basket of fruit
and a rug for the floor and a boat with an oar
and a rocking chair and a stuffed teddy bear
and a frying pan in the moving van.
   What else did you see?
   Tell, tell, tell.

47

Well, I saw a lamp with a shade and a jug of lemonade
and a steamer trunk and a double-decker bunk
and a TV set and a Ping-Pong net
and a leather boot and a basket of fruit
and a rug for the floor and a boat with an oar
and a rocking chair and a stuffed teddy bear
and a frying pan in the moving van.
What else did you see?
Tell, tell, tell.

Well, since you ask it:
I saw a wicker basket
and a violin and a rolling pin and a vegetable bin
and a lamp with a shade and a jug of lemonade
   and a garden spade
      and a steamer trunk and a double-decker bunk
         and a Chinese model junk
      and a TV set and a Ping-Pong net
         and a framed silhouette
      and a leather boot and a basket of fruit
         and a baseball suit
      and a rug for the floor and a boat with an oar
         and a knob for a door
and a rocking chair and a stuffed teddy bear
   and plastic dinnerware
and an electric fan and a bent tin can
   and a frying pan and
         THAT'S ALL I SAW IN THE MOVING VAN.

After you have read this poem by Eve Merriam once or twice, you might like to think of *actions* to do as you say your lines.

The pictures on these pages will give you some ideas.

Learn your own lines and then see how far you can get without looking at your books. Help each other to remember the words by doing the actions.

Make up your own "What did you see? Tell, tell, tell" poem, for example:

On Saturday night I went to the fair.
You'll never, never guess what I saw there.

What did you see?
Tell, tell, tell.

Well,
I saw . . . .

STORY TALK WITH
READERS AND WRITERS

Shirley Hughes began to write and illustrate picture books when her own three children were very young. You will find her drawings in over 200 books for children of all ages. Her own stories are usually about amusing, everyday happenings in families.

Shirley thinks it is a pity that older children do not have many pictures in books that are written for them. She says: "Little children get large full-colour picture books, young readers get one or two illustrations each chapter and older children get no pictures at all." That is why the books she has written for your age group have pictures on every page.

"My older brother recommended this book. I like funny books. This is about a professor's inventions which don't work. I have a good selection of books at home which I like to read again. I get some from the local library. I enjoy reading in the early morning in bed."   Matthew (age 8)

"*A lamp for the lambchops* is a thin book so I read it in one go. It started off exciting and it was good right to the end. The best bit was where Stanley and Arthur wanted to fly and the genie granted their wish. Now I'd like to read *Flat Stanley* by the same author."   Kirandeep (age 7)

"I'm in the middle of three books. I keep them under my pillow. I start one book, stop at chapter two and then pick up the other one. I never get the characters mixed up. Under my pillow at the moment I have *Ramona and Beezus*, *The giraffe, the pelly and me* and a picture book called *The twelve dancing princesses*."   Gayle-Louise (age 8)

"I started to love reading because I was given lots of books. It started me to read and when I could read properly I really enjoyed them. I like adventure stories which are exciting and thrilling. I want to be a writer or a nurse. I read whenever I have spare time . . . in my bedroom . . . anywhere as long as I can read . . . even in a dustbin."   Ruth (age 7)

We asked Gary, aged nine, what he remembered about being read to when he was little. He said: "Dad read us stories from the books he had when he was young. We didn't always get the story but it didn't matter. It was a nice thought. He did it in the hope that we would drop to sleep but it didn't work!"

Gary talked about television:

"You can go outside with a book. Television makes you lazy. Television reads for you; I want to read for myself."

STORY STARTERS

On the next seven pages, there are some book covers or pictures and the beginnings of the books – "Story starters".

Read the "Story starters" aloud to each other.

Which one would you most like to go on reading to find out what happens next?

Start by saying what kind of story it is.

Is it one of these?

	1	2	3	4	5	6	7	8	9
SCARY	✓								
FUNNY	✓								
ADVENTURE									
ANIMAL									
FANTASY	✓								
FAIRY									
STORY/ POEM									
FACTUAL									
MYSTERY									

We guess that story number 1 might be a funny, scary, fantasy story, so we have put ticks by these words in column 1.

Copy the table on to a sheet of paper and read the "starters" again. Make guesses about what kind of story you think each might be. Then put ticks by those words in the right columns. You can get together in your groups and try making up the rest of each story.

You may be able to find some of these stories in your book corner or library. Do they go on the way you thought they would?

If you have already read and enjoyed any of these books, try to persuade a friend to read it.

1 *Knock knock who's there?* Sally Grindley

STORY TALK

KNOCK KNOCK
Who's there?

I'm a great big GORILLA
with fat furry arms
and huge white teeth.

When you let me in,
I'm going to hug your breath away!

2 *Whodunnit?* Caroline Browne

This is the mystery of the Big Butterly Burglary. Can you help to solve it? If you are good at looking for clues, you can help. If not, just listen to the story.

It all started the day the Mouse family went down to the station to spot trains.

They made a day of it and took a picnic. Tilly and Tom spotted plenty of trains, but they spotted something else as well. All mice are curiously curious, they love to poke and pry.

So as soon as Tilly and Tom had gobbled their cheese they poked and pried in the waiting room. Behind the iron stove Tom spotted a bundle of newspaper, and when they poked and pried into *that* what should roll out but a sparkling ruby ring!

What a spot!

Off they went to the police station.

P.C. Dog looked at the ring. "That is a worthless object," he proclaimed. "It isn't worth tuppence."

P.C. Dog couldn't see things even when they were right under his nose, let alone behind his left ear.

Tilly and Tom spotted something, though. Can you?

3   *The trouble with Gran* Babette Cole

The trouble with Gran is ...
... secretly ...
She's an alien!
None of the other OAP's suspected a thing ...
... until our teacher tried to organise an outing for them, to Wethorp, as our school project!

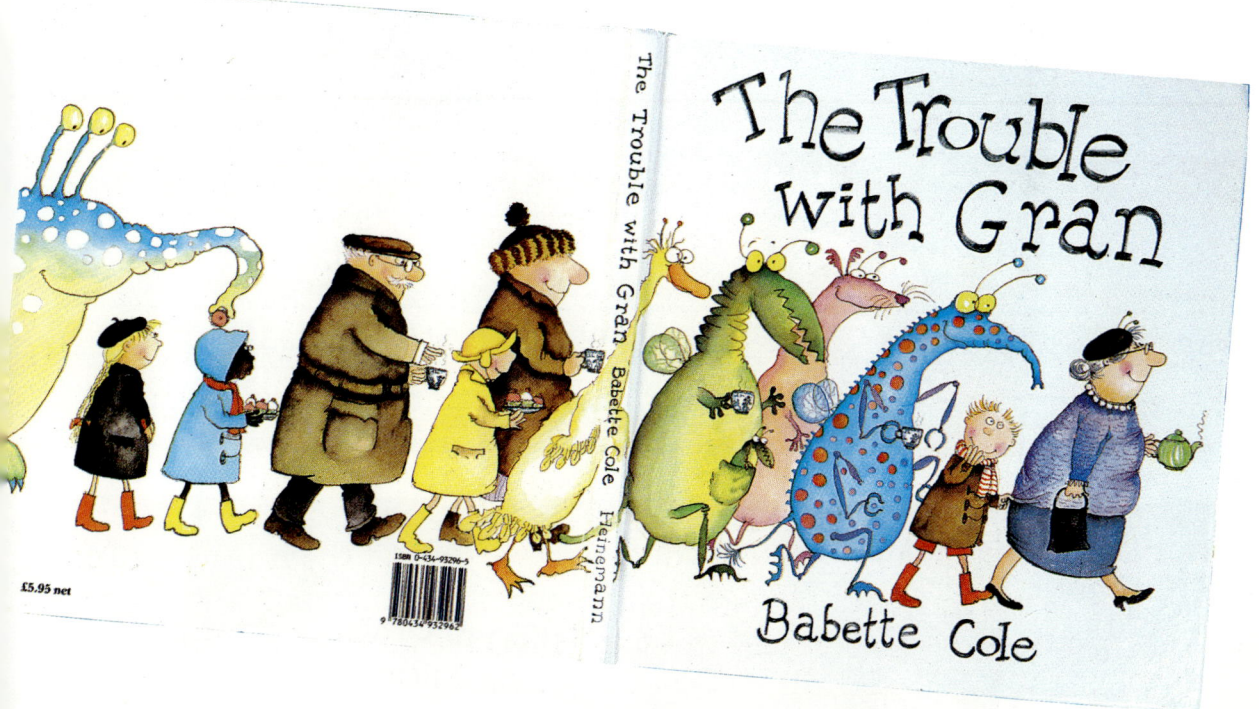

4 *Angry Arthur* Hiawyn Oram

Once there was a boy called Arthur.

He wanted to stay up and watch the western on T.V.

"No," said his mother, "it's too late. Go to bed."

"I'll get angry," said Arthur.

"Get angry," said his mother.

So he did. Very, very angry.

He got so angry that his anger became a stormcloud exploding thunder and lightning and hailstones.

"That's enough," said his mother.

But it wasn't.

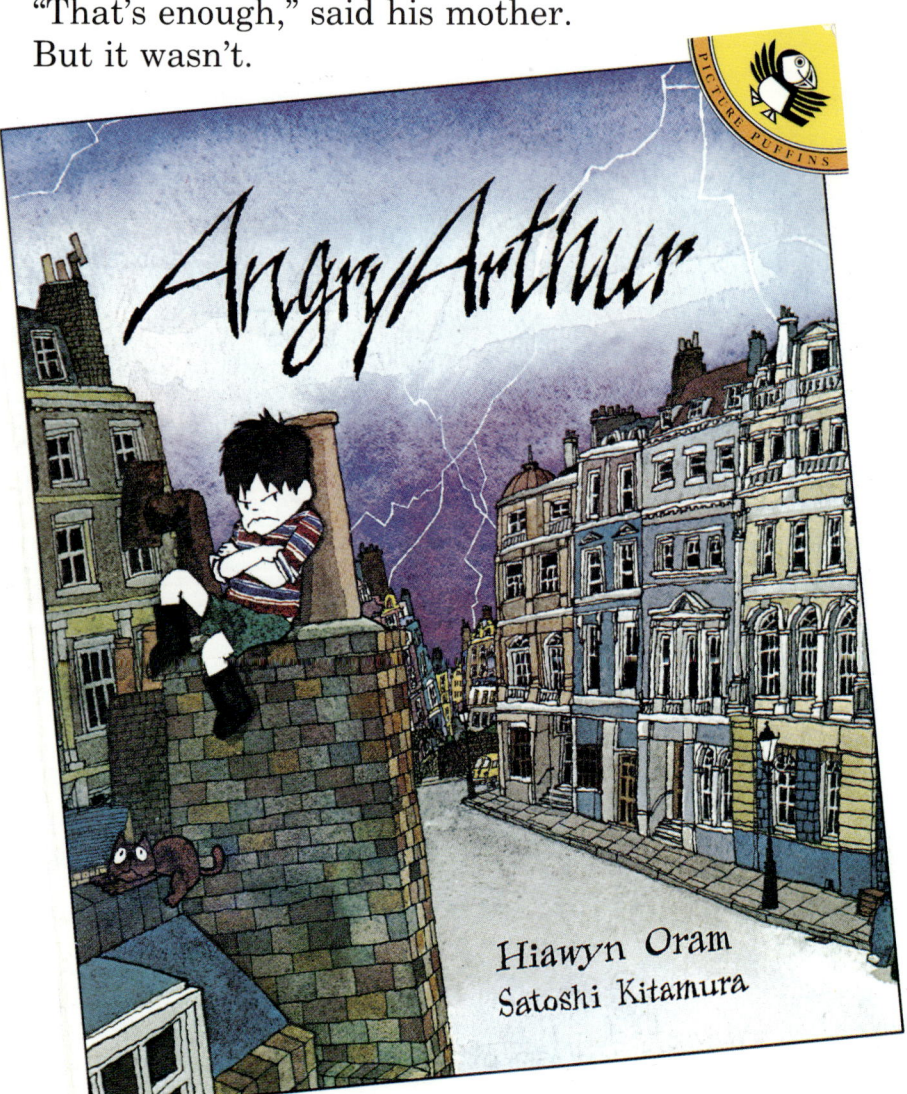

5 *The conker as hard as a diamond* Chris Powling

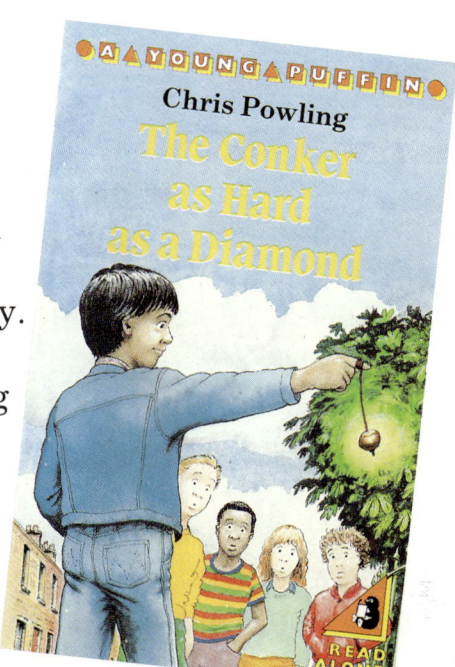

Hello!

    This is the story of Little Alpesh and the conker as hard as a diamond. It's rather a *strange* story. To tell you the truth I'm not sure I believe it myself – and I'm telling it. Let's hope you're better at believing things than I am.

6 *The spider* Margaret Lane

A lot of people are afraid of spiders, which is rather foolish of them. If there were no spiders our life, both indoors and out, would be very nasty. Scientists have discovered that the flies and other tiresome insects that spiders get rid of every year weigh more than all the people in the world!

7 *Who's a clever girl then?* Rose Impey

If you think this is the kind of
story where five children, armed
only with a bucket and spade,
catch a dangerous band of
smugglers, you'd be wrong. And if
you think this is the kind of story
where a poor, helpless little girl is
captured by a terrible gang of cut-
throat pirates ... you'd still be
wrong, but a lot closer. Now, those
are all the hints I'm going to give
you. To find what happens, you'd
better read on ...

Once upon a time, and not so
very long ago, a little girl was
walking to school. She was a
sensible sort of girl,

8 *"Rooms to let" from Leaf magic* Margaret Mahy

Mr Murgatroyd hung a sign on the front of his house:

ROOMS TO LET

He was small and shrivelled and as bitter as medicine because
of the mean, hard life he had led, and he talked to himself
because of his loneliness.

"How much shall I charge for my rooms?" he asked himself.
He chuckled. "*Too* much!" he declared so sharply that the key
rattled in the lock, probably from fear.

One day Mr Murgatroyd heard an unusual-sounding knock on
the door.

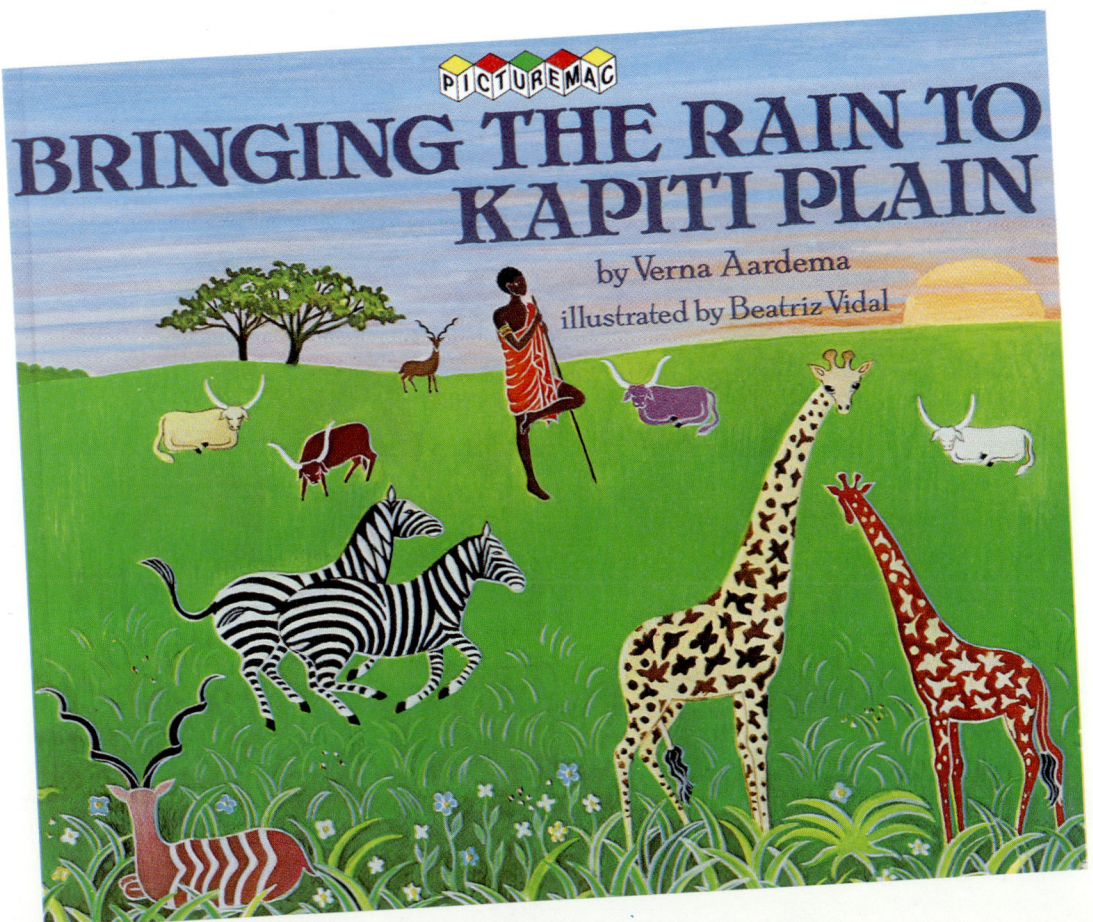
9 *Bringing the rain to Kapiti Plain*
Verna Aardema/Beatriz Vidal

This is the great
  Kapiti Plain,
All fresh and green
  from the African rains –
A sea of grass for the
  ground birds to nest in,
And patches of shade for
  wild creatures to rest in;
With acacia trees for
  giraffes to browse on,

And grass for the herdsmen
  to pasture their cows on.
But one year the rains
  were so very belated,
That all of the big wild
  creatures migrated.
Then Ki-pat helped to end
  that terrible drought –
And this story tells
  how it all came about!

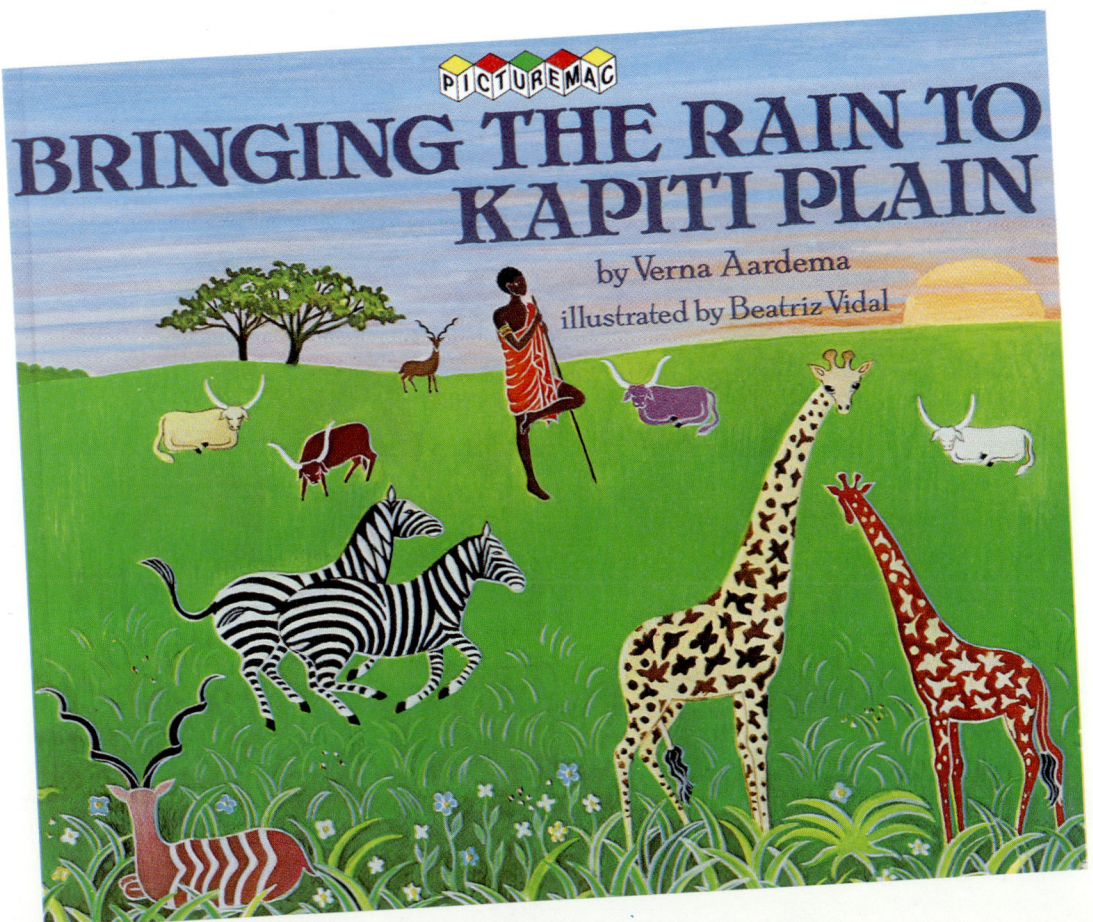

PICTUREMAC

BRINGING THE RAIN TO KAPITI PLAIN

by Verna Aardema
illustrated by Beatriz Vidal

EVERY SORT OF STORY

SPRING FEVER

In this part of the book there are some complete stories and poems for you to read. When you have read them all, you could make your own class "Every sort of story" chart. Make a big poster like the chart on page 52. Instead of the numbers at the top of each column, put the titles of different stories that you liked. Talk about what sort of story each one is, and put ticks in the boxes.

Some stories are best enjoyed when they are read aloud in small groups. You will need six readers for this next one. Look closely at the "starter". It's from *Another helping of chips* by Shirley Hughes.

Read the words in the bubbles to find out how Chips, his grandpa and the cat feel about what Mum is planning to do.

Now let the story bubble over, with Chips, Grandpa, Mum, Jessie, Albert the cat and one person who reads the bits outside the bubbles and makes the sounds.

Perfect peace ... rudely shattered!

But help is on the way . . .

EVERY SORT OF STORY

From now on I'm going to do just as I want!

No more proper meals. You can be as messy as you like.

I've got to go home for supper now, Chips.

Goodnight, Jessie!

Just think of it, Albert, No more awful spring-cleaning!

Chips! It's supper-time!

I'm not coming!

Come on, it's sausages and beans, your favourite.

Albert and I are staying HERE!

But it'll be dark soon!

NO!

Oh, very well, then!

Leave us alone. We're camping!

Slam!

Good. She's gone indoors!

Later that night:

Mum? Are you awake?

Come on, inside!

Is that you, Chips?

We've decided not to camp out, after all!

Albert was a bit NERVOUS of the dark.

...so I think perhaps we'll wait till the summer comes.

Good idea, Chips. I've finished the spring-cleaning, anyway.

How are you liking living in a tent, Chips?

It must be such FUN!

Well, er, now that things are back to normal at home, Albert and I have decided to POSTPONE our plans for a little while...

65

CATALOGUE CATS

If you have filled in the poem on page 24, you will know that cats have the habit of jumping into all kinds of words. This time you open a catalogue and the cats jump out ... or so Julian says to his little brother Huey, in 'Catalogue cats' by Ann Cameron.

"Would you boys like to plant gardens?" my father said.

"Yes," we said.

"Good!" said my father. "I'll order a catalogue."

So it was settled. But afterwards, Huey said to me, "What's a catalogue?"

"A catalogue," I said, "is where cats come from. It's a big book full of pictures of hundreds and hundreds of cats. And when you open it up, all the cats jump out and start running around."

"I don't believe you," Huey said.

"It's true," I said.

"But why would Dad be sending for that catalogue cat book?"

"The cats help with the garden," I said.

"I don't believe you," Huey said.

"It's true," I said. "You open the catalogue, and the cats jump out. Then they run outside and work in the garden. White cats dig up the ground with their claws. Black cats brush the ground smooth with their tails. Yellow and brown cats roll on the seeds to push them underground so they can grow."

"I don't believe you," Huey said. "Cats don't act like that."

"Of course," I said, "*ordinary* cats don't act like that. That's why you have to get them specially – catalogue cats."

"Really?" Huey said.

"Really," I said.

"I'm going to ask Dad about it," Huey said.

"You ask Dad about everything," I said. "Don't you think it's time you learned something on your own for a change?"

Huey looked hurt. "I do learn things by myself," he said. "I wonder when the catalogue will come."

"Soon," I said.

The next morning Huey woke me up. "I dreamed about the catalogue cats!" he said. "Only in my dream the yellow and brown ones were washing the windows and painting the house! You don't suppose they could do that, do you?"

"No, they can't do that, Huey," I said. "They don't have a way to hold rags and paintbrushes."

"I suppose not," Huey said.

Every day Huey asked my father if the catalogue had come.

"Not yet," my father kept saying. He was very pleased that Huey was so interested in the garden.

Huey dreamed about the catalogue cats again. A whole team of them was carrying a giant pumpkin to the house. One had his teeth around the stem. The others were pushing it with their shoulders and their heads.

"Do you think that's what they really do, Julian?" Huey said.

"Yes, they do that," I said.

Two weeks went by.

"Well, Huey and Julian," my father said, "today is the big day. The catalogue is here."

"The catalogue is here! The catalogue is here! The catalogue is here!" Huey said. He was dancing and twirling around.

I was thinking about going somewhere else.

"What's the matter, Julian?" my father said. "Don't you want to see the catalogue?"

"Oh, yes, I – want to see it," I said.

My father had the catalogue under his arm. The three of us sat down on the couch.

"Open it!" Huey said.

My father opened the catalogue.

Inside were bright pictures of flowers and vegetables. The catalogue company would send you the seeds, and you could grow the flowers and vegetables.

Huey started turning the pages faster and faster. "Where are the cats? Where are the cats?" he kept saying.

"What cats?" my father said.

Huey started to cry.

My father looked at me. "Julian," he said, "please tell me what is going on."

"Huey thought catalogues were books with cats in them. Catalogue cats," I said.

Huey sobbed. "Julian told me! Special cats – cats that work in gardens! White ones – they dig up the dirt. Black ones – they brush the ground with their tails. Yellow and brown ones – they roll on the seeds." Huey was crying harder than ever.

"Julian!" said my father.

"Yes," I said. When my father's voice gets loud, mine gets so small I can only whisper.

"Julian," my father said, "didn't you tell Huey that catalogue cats are invisible?"

"No," I said.

"Julian told me they jumped out of catalogues! He said they jump out and work in gardens. As soon as you get the catalogue, they go to work."

"Well," said my father, "that's very ignorant. Julian has never had a garden before in his life. I wouldn't trust a person who has never had a garden in his life to tell me about catalogue cats. Would you?"

"No," Huey said slowly. He was still crying a little.

My father pulled out his handkerchief and gave it to Huey. "Now, blow your nose and listen to me," my father said.

Huey blew his nose and sat up straight on the couch. I sat back and tried to be as small as I could.

"First of all," said my father, "a lot of people have wasted a lot of time trying to see catalogue cats. It's a waste of time because catalogue cats are the fastest animals alive. No one is as quick as a catalogue cat. It may be that they really *are* visible and that they just move so quickly you can't see them. But you can feel them. When you look for a catalogue cat over your right shoulder, you can feel that he is climbing the tree above your left ear. When you turn fast and look at the tree, you can feel that he has jumped out and landed behind your back. And then sometimes you feel all the little hairs on your backbone quiver – that's when you know a catalogue cat is laughing at you and telling you that you are wasting your time.

"Catalogue cats love gardens, and they love to work in gardens. However, they will only do half the work. If they are in a garden where people don't do any work, the catalogue cats will not do any work either. But if they are in a garden where people work hard, all the work will go twice as fast because of the catalogue cats."

"When you were a boy and had a garden," Huey said, "did your garden have catalogue cats?"

"Yes," my father said, "my garden had catalogue cats."

"And were they your friends?" Huey said.

"Well," my father said, "they like people, but they move too fast to make friends."

"There's one more thing," my father said. "Catalogue cats aren't *in* garden catalogues, and no one can order catalogue cats. Catalogue cats are only *around* the companies the catalogues come from. You don't order them, you request them."

"I can write up a request," I said.

"Huey can do that very well, I'm sure," my father said, "if he would like to. Would you like to, Huey?"

Huey said he would.

My father got a piece of paper and pencil.

And Huey wrote it all down:

REQUESTED
I dozen catalogue cats
all varieties
WHOEVER
wants to come
IS WELCOME

WHO'S THE STRONGEST?

Do you know the story of the contest between the Sun and the North Wind? Do you know who won? Here's a chance to read that story, along with one about another contest. In the second story, Tom Poker speaks to Ice, Sun, Cloud, Wind, Hill and Tree to find out who is the strongest. Which one do you think it is?

One morning the North Wind and the Sun saw a horseman wearing a new cloak.

"That young man looks very pleased with his new cloak," said the North Wind. "But I could easily blow it off his back if I wanted to."

"I don't think you could," said the Sun. "But let us both try to do it. You can try first."

The North Wind began to blow and blow and blow.
People had to chase after their hats.
Leaves were blown from the trees.
All the animals were frightened.
The ships in the harbour were sunk.
The North Wind blew with all his might, but it was no use, for the horseman just pulled his cloak more tightly around him.

"My turn now," cried the Sun.

And as he gave out his gentle heat, insects hummed and flowers opened.

The birds began to sing.
The animals lay down to sleep.
And the people came out to gossip.

The horseman began to feel very hot, and when he came to a river he took off his clothes and went in for a swim. So the Sun was able to achieve by warmth and gentleness what the North Wind in all his strength and fury could not do.

That story was an old story, retold by Brian Wildsmith. Now read another story about a contest. It's by Alan Garner, and it's called *Tom Poker*.

One winter's day, Tom Poker went out chopping wood. (It was a hard winter, and times were bad.)

He'd not gone far when he trod on some ice; and he slipped and he fell, and it took his breath away. Tom Poker said to the ice, "Ice, ice," said Tom Poker, "you've knocked me down. You must be strong."

"I am," said the ice. "You may depend on it."

73

"But when sun comes, you run away," said Tom Poker.

"Oh," said the ice, "that's very true."

"Well, then," said Tom Poker; "sun is stronger."

And the ice said, "He is, seemingly."

Tom Poker said to the sun, "Sun, sun," said Tom Poker, "are you strong?"

"I am," said the sun. "You may depend on it."

"But when cloud comes, you hide," said Tom Poker.

"Oh," said the sun, "that's very true."

"Well, then," said Tom Poker; "cloud is stronger."

And the sun said, "She is, seemingly."

Tom Poker said to the cloud, "Cloud, cloud," said Tom Poker, "are you strong?"

"I am," said the cloud. "You may depend on it."

"But when wind comes, you're blown to bits," said Tom Poker.

"Oh," said the cloud, "that's very true."

"Well, then," said Tom Poker; "wind is stronger."

And the cloud said, "She is, seemingly."

Tom Poker said to the wind, "Wind, wind," said Tom Poker, "are you strong?"

"I am," said the wind. "You may depend on it."

"But can you shift hill?" said Tom Poker.

"I can't, " said the wind. "That's very true."

"Well, then," said Tom Poker; "hill is stronger."

And the wind said, "He is, seemingly."

Tom Poker said to the hill, "Hill, hill," said Tom Poker, "are you strong?"

"I am," said the hill. "You may depend on it."

"But can you stand on tree?" said Tom Poker.

"I can't," said the hill.

"But tree can stand on you," said Tom Poker.

"She can," said the hill. "That's very true."

"Well, then," said Tom Poker; "tree is stronger."

And the hill said, "She is, seemingly."

Tom Poker said to the tree, "Tree, tree," said Tom Poker, "are you strong?"

"I am," said the tree. "You may depend on it."

Tom Poker swung his axe. "Then have that! and have that! and have that!" said Tom Poker. "Have that! And now who is strong?" said Tom Poker.

But the tree said never a word; for he'd chopped the tree down.

"Me, seemingly! Strongest of all!" said Tom Poker. And he gave a hop. But he hopped on the ice, and he slipped; and the ice took his breath away from Tom Poker.

Now that you have read both stories aloud you might have some good ideas for a contest story of your own. Try to imagine a fight between Winter and Spring. What do you think they might argue about?

75

FRIENDLY WARNINGS TO DARK

After reading "Friendly warnings" (page 10), two eight-year-old poets wrote these friendly warnings to Dark:

Sarah's
Friendly
Warning

Listen Dark
If you want to stay up
Lo . . . . nger
Don't let
the sun-
shine
in .

Dawn's
Friendly
Warning

Listen Dark
Put on the Light
You're the nearest!

POEM ABOUT THE SUN SLINKING OFF AND PINNING UP A NOTICE

The friendly warnings to Dark reminded us
of this poem by Roger McGough:

the sun
hasn't got me fooled
not for a minute
just when
you're beginning to believe
that   grass is green
and   skies are blue
and   colour is king
hey   ding a ding ding
and

      a

          host

              of

                  other

                      golden

                          etceteras

before you know where you are
he's slunk off somewhere
and pinned up a notice saying:

MOON

77

THE LONGEST JOURNEY IN THE WORLD

When the poet Michael Rosen and his brother were children and shared a bedroom, they used to play a scary game called "Last one into bed".

In this poem Michael Rosen tells us how he felt when he lost the race and had to turn off the light.

See if you can find an interesting way of reading the poem aloud in pairs.

"Last one into bed
has to switch out the light."
It's just the same every night.
There's a race.
I'm ripping off my trousers and shirt,
he's kicking off his shoes and socks.

"My sleeve's stuck."
"This button's too big for its button-hole."
"Have you hidden my pyjamas?"
"Keep your hands off mine."

If you win
you get where it's safe
before the darkness comes –
but if you lose
if you're last
you know what you've got coming up is
the journey from the light switch to your bed
It's the Longest Journey in the World.

"You're last tonight," my brother says.
And he's right.

There is nowhere so dark
as that room in the moment
after I've switched out the light.

There is nowhere so full of dangerous things,
things that love dark places,
things that breathe only when you breathe
and hold their breath when I hold mine.

So I have to say:
"I'm not scared."
That face, grinning in the pattern on the
wall, isn't a face –
"I'm not scared."
That prickle on the back of my neck
is only the label on my pyjama jacket –
"I'm not scared."
That moaning-moaning is nothing
but water in a pipe –
"I'm not scared."

Everything's going to be just fine
as soon as I get into that bed of mine.
Such a terrible shame
it's always the same
it takes so long
it takes so long
it takes so long
to get there.

From the light switch
to my bed
it's the Longest Journey in the World.

Have you a story to tell about your longest
journey when you were frightened?

79

ACKNOWLEDGEMENTS

The authors and publishers wish to thank the following who have kindly given permission for the use of copyright material: Andersen Press Ltd. for illustrations and extracts from *Angry Arthur* by Hiawyn Oram and Satoshi Kitamura, 1982, and *If at first you do not see* by Ruth Brown, 1982; The Bodley Head Ltd. for an illustration from *Where the wild things are* by Maurice Sendak, 1967; an extract and illustrations from 'Spring fever' from *Another helping of chips* written and illustrated by Shirley Hughes, 1987; and 'Mouth open, story jump out' from *Say it again Granny* by John Agard; Jonathan Cape Ltd. for 'Batty' from *A light in the attic* by Shel Silverstein; illustrations and extract from *Where's Julius?* written and illustrated by John Burningham, 1986; 'Poem about the sun slinking off and pinning up a notice' from *Watchwords* by Roger McGough; and the front cover, illustration and text from *Whodunnit?*, illustrated by Caroline Browne, story by Helen Cresswell, 1986; Collins Publishers for an illustration and text from *The gingerbread rabbit* by Randall Jarrell, illustrated by Garth Williams, Lions. Copyright © 1964, text by Randall Jarrell, illustration by Garth Williams; 'Our hamster's life' from *Rabbiting on* by Kit Wright, Young Lions. Copyright © 1978 by Kit Wright; 'Tom Poker' from *A bag of moonshine* by Alan Garner. Copyright © 1986 by Alan Garner; and the front cover and extract from *The spider* by Margaret Lane, illustrated by Barbara Firth, Picture Lions. Copyright © 1982, text by Margaret Lane, illustrated by Barbara Firth; Judy Daish Associates Ltd. on behalf of the author for 'The park' by Olive Dehn; Andre Deutsch Ltd. for 'The longest journey in the world' from *You can't catch me* by Michael Rosen, 1981; Robert Froman for 'Friendly warning'. Copyright © 1987 by Robert Froman; Victor Gollancz Ltd. for illustrations and text from 'Catalogue cats' from *The Julian stories* by Ann Cameron, illustrated by Ann Strugnell. Illustrations © 1981 by Ann Strugnell; Hamish Hamilton Ltd. for the front cover and extracts from *A bit of give and take* by Bernard Ashley, 1984; and illustration and extracts from *Knock knock who's there?* by Sally Grindley, illustrated by Anthony Browne, 1985; William Heinemann Ltd. for the front cover and extract from *Who's a clever girl then?* by Rose Impey, illustrated by Andre Amstrutz, 1985; text and covers from *The trouble with Gran* by Babette Cole. Copyright © Babette Cole 1987; Jean Kenward for 'Gerbil'; Macmillan Children's Books for illustrations and extracts from *Bringing the rain to Kapiti Plain* by Verna Aardema, illustrated by Beatriz Vidal, and *On the way home*, written and illustrated by Jill Murphy; Julia MacRae Books for an extract from *Bridget and William* by Jane Gardam, Blackbird Series. Copyright © 1981 by Jane Gardam; Methuen Children's Books for an extract from *The owl who was afraid of the dark* by Jill Tomlinson, 1986; Oxford University Press for illustrations and extract from *The North Wind and the Sun*, written and illustrated by Brian Wildsmith, 1964; Penguin Books Ltd. for the front cover and extract from *The conker as hard as a diamond* by Chris Powling, illustrated by Jon Riley, Puffin Books. Copyright © 1984 by Jon Riley and Chris Powling; the front cover and double page spread from *Moonlight* by Jan Ormerod, Puffin Books. Copyright © 1982 by Jan Ormerod; and 'Someone stole the ...' from *Gargling with jelly* by Brian Patten, Kestrel Books. Copyright © 1985 by Brian Patten; Marian Reiner for 'Frying pan in the moving van' from *A word or two with you* by Eve Merriam.

Every effort has been made to trace all the copyright holders but if any have been inadvertently overlooked the publishers will be pleased to make the necessary arrangement at the first opportunity.

First published 1989

Published by
MACMILLAN EDUCATION LTD
Houndmills, Basingstoke, Hampshire RG21 2XS
and London
Companies and representatives
throughout the world

Designed by Roger Walker/Linda Hardaker

Printed in Hong Kong

ISBN 0–333–45387–5

Illustrations: Shirley Bellwood pages 39, 40, 41, 76; Val Biro pages 8, 9, 24, 25, 42, 43; Roma Bishop pages 5, 6, 7, 74, 75; Kim Blundell pages 46, 47, 48, 49; Ian Foulis & Associates pages 10, 11, 38, 52; Julie Hughes pages 26, 27, 28, 32, 33, 34; Ken Morton pages 30, 78, 79; Steve Smallman pages 22, 23, 77; Joyce Smith and David Dowland pages 11, 35, 36, 37, 66, 67, 68, 69, 70, 71. Cover illustration: Lynne Willey. Contents page: Steve Smallman.